The LAWN Care Guide

The shortest most impactful manual for lawn care systems and tools.

Brought to you by

Table of Contents

Contents

COPYRIGHT

© Copyright 2018 - All rights reserved.

derived from various sources. Please consult a licensed professional before attempting any techniques outlined in this book.

Chapter One

Introduction

What is Lawn Painting?

Lawn paint has has been a landscaper's secret weapon at athletic fields and golf courses for years, but the current drought, bad weather and climate change is prompting homeowners to consider lawn painting as a way to maintain a emerald green lawn when water is in abondent or is in short supply. Good ⏍uality lawn paint is formulated to be biodegradable and safe for the environment. Once the lawn paint dries, the painted turf is safe for children and pets. The color won't run on dewy mornings, a rainfall won't wash it off, and it won't rub off on your clothes. Painted grass usually retains its color two to three months and sometimes much longer. However, fre⏍uency of mowing, type of grass, weather and rate of new growth all affect the color. In some cases, the color may fade in two to three weeks.

Lawn Care is Not Just Cutting the Grass

Mowing a lawn is certainly important to having a nice landscaped yard. But, it isn't the only thing you need to tend to. The truth is that Lawn Care encompasses much more than cutting the grass, and to obtain a well-kept lawn, you will also need to focus on some more of the finer details of landscaping. That means that you will eventually have to get off of your riding lawn mowers and break out the weed trimmers and the lawn grass seed. You can also spray some liquid lawn fertilizer, hunt for some good flower garden ideas and maybe give some thought to different styles of wooden fences and other landscaping accessories.

The first thing you will want to do is know what your lawn needs. From your lawns health, cutting your grass is usually the first step in Lawn Care. After that, you need to do some trimming of weeds and over growth as well as some edging. After this, you can better access your lawns needs. You might need some simple weed and feed mixture, or you lawn may need more extensive work such as reseeding or even sodding.

After you have addressed the health of your lawn, it is time to give it some sprucing up. Planting flowers is always a great way to add some color and some beauty to a homes lawn. Lawn Care from a decorative prospective does not has to end there, however. Dressing up a backyard patio or walkway is a good way to add to your lawns overall appeal. Other landscaping features like decorative fences, planters and outdoor lighting are ways you can really punch up the look of you homes exterior and increase the curb appeal as well. Fountains and other water features can make your yard look beautiful as well.

There are many things that can add to a homes landscaped design, and it is different for everyone. Fortunately, there are plenty of options. However, before you start dressing up your lawn, make sure that it is healthy. A beautiful garden or some slick landscaping features will not do much if your lawn is dying or being chocked off by weeds and overgrowth. With a healthy lawn, not only will your grass look good, it will also help you to maximize all the wonderful landscaping features that would look so good in your yard.

How to Paint Lawn Turf

So if you would like to give the DIY lawn painting a try, purchase lawn paint at a garden center or landscaping service. Don't scrimp. Good paint is easier to apply. It will look better and last longer. Paint your lawn on a dry, sunny, windless day. Mow your lawn and rake up grass clippings and yard debris. If you've watered the grass recently, let it dry before you paint because the paint won't stick to damp grass. Use plastic sheeting to cover anything you don't want to paint, including brick or concrete patios, driveways, garden mulch and fence posts. Secure the plastic with masking tape. Unless your lawn is huge, you can apply lawn paint using a hand sprayer with a fine spray nozzle. A pump sprayer works better for larger lawns, while a spray paint system is more efficient for super large or commercial landscapes. With the nozzle about 7 inches from the turf, apply the paint in a back and forth motion to ensure all sides of the grass are evenly colored. If any paint lands where you don't want it, remove it immediately with ammonia-based window spray and a wire brush.

Lawn Care Basics

A beautiful, well-maintained lawn is the pride of most neighborhoods. The way your grass looks depends on the way that you take care of it. There are some basic things that you can do to help keep your grass healthy and beautiful. Mowing, watering, feeding, aerating and scarifying are all important steps to follow for basic lawn care. The well cared for lawn can also add value to your home if you are trying to sell. Curb appeal is very important to homeowners so read on to help learn the basics of lawn care.

- **Mowing**

-

When mowing your lawn the most important thing to remember is the height of the grass. You should never cut more than one-third of the height of the grass blades. Make sure to always leave the grass clippings on the yard because this will provide fertilizer for your grass. You should be mowing your lawn at least once a week but an ideal situation would be mowing more than once a week. Keep your mower blade sharp and never mow in the same direction. You should also never mow your lawn when it is wet. Wet mowing will cause clumps of clippings and that can breed bacteria. Choose your type of mower by the size of lawn you have. A small lawn that can be done in half an hour or less is best done with a walking mower. Larger lawns will re?uire a ride-on mower.

- **Watering**

Watering your grass is important to keep the grass healthy and looking beautiful. When you water your grass it should be done early in the day. Avoid watering your grass too frequently. When the yard is watered be sure that it is done so there is a good soaking so it will not have to be done for a while. Watch the weather and if it is going to rain then you don't need to do any watering.

- **Feeding**

Lawn feed is another important part of maintenance to keep your lawn looking beautiful and make it the envy of the neighborhood. Before feeding your soil you should have it tested to see which nutrients that is missing from the structure of it and what you need to be adding. In the spring you should be adding a spring/summer fertilizer. This is a lawn feed that is high in nitrogen and is low in phosphates. In the autumn, you will use a lawn feed that has low nitrogen and high phosphates. There is also a mixture of fine sand, ammonium and iron sulfate that can be put on your yard to prevent the growth of weeds and moss. The sand is usually applied in the late spring.

- **Aerating**

Aerating is usually done with a piece of e?uipment known as an aerator. The lawn aerator is run over the grass the same way as a mower but instead of cutting the grass this piece of e?uipment actually pulls out plugs of dirt and grass. Aerating will help your grass build a better root system and will help with compacted soil and thatch grass. A aerator is a good investment for the care of your yard and to help your grass look healthy. Leave the soil plugs on the grass so that they can provide fertilization as they decompose. Aerating can also be done by wearing cleats onto your lawn and just walking around.

- **Scarifying**

Scarifying is like exfoliation for your yard. You are going to take away all the bad stuff and get down to the nice, new, healthy grass. Scarifying your yard is removing the dead material from your grass. You can do this by using a rake but a scarifier can reach further than the rake and can remove more waste. The scarifier reaches between the grass blades and removes the decaying matter without damaging the blades of grass. Using the scarifier is as easy as using a rake. Before you start scarifying you need to remove any living weed, fungus or invasive plants. You also need to kill any moss that is growing in the lawn. Autumn is the best time to do the scarifying because the soil is moist and warm. The reason that this needs to be done is because the dead and decaying debris that is laying on the grass will eventually smother it and kill it out. Using the scarifier will keep your grass healthy and disease free.

Your lawn is the first thing that a visitor to your home will see. This is the first impression that they get of you so it is up to you to make it a good one. It may take an investment of some time to make this first impression a good one but it will be worth it. A well-maintained lawn shows that you care about your surroundings.

- **Lawn Watering Guidelines**

Here are the basic guidelines for when and how to water your lawn more effectively. When to Water Lawns The best time to water lawns is when the grass begins to show signs of stress. A stressed lawn will look slightly wilted with a bluish-green tint instead of its usual emerald green. If footprints or lawnmower tracks remain on the grass 30 minutes after you mow or walk across it, the lawn is stressed. You can test soil moisture by inserting a screwdriver, trowel or similar object into the grass. If the ground is so hard that the screwdriver doesn't slide in easily, the soil is too dry. Always confirm that the lawn needs water by testing the soil before irrigating; hot, dry weather can cause the grass to look stressed even when the soil is still moist. If the grass looks stressed and the soil are still damp, spray the grass with water for no more than 15 seconds. This ⬚uick burst of water isn't considered irrigating because it doesn't wet the soil; it provides just enough moisture to cool the grass and relieve stress. How to Water a Lawn It's difficult to know how much to water a lawn because the amount depends on several factors, including type of grass, climate, soil type, and use. Experimentation is the best way to learn. For example, apply about ½ inch of water if your soil is sandy, and approximately an inch if your soil is fine textured, clay based or heavy. (An inexpensive rain gauge is the easiest way to know how much water you've applied.) This amount of water should soak the soil to a depth of 4 to 6 inches, but you should test the soil with a trowel or screwdriver to know for sure. If water begins to run off before you've irrigated the recommended amount, allow the water to soak in, and then finish watering. (Heavy soil should be watered with a slower rate to help prevent runoff.) Once you've done this a few times, you'll have a better idea about how to water a lawn efficiently.

Additional Watering Lawn Care Tips

Water deeply but only when the grass shows signs of stress; deep, infrequent irrigation creates strong, drought-tolerant roots. Never water every day; watering too frequently encourages shallow, weak roots and unhealthy grass. For a healthy lawn and sturdy roots, wait as long as possible before watering and don't bother watering if the weather report predicts rain. Water early in the morning to minimize evaporation. An inexpensive sprinkler timer is an option if you're an not an early bird. Irrigate only the stressed areas of your lawn, as grass doesn't always dry evenly. Areas with sandy soil or near driveways and sidewalks tend to dry out faster.

Homemade Fertilizers for Lawns

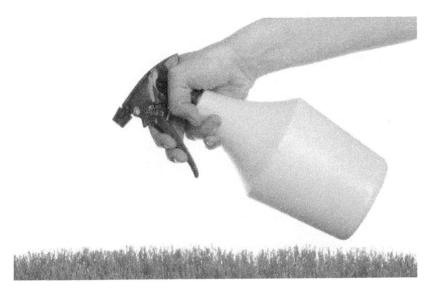

There are some key ingredients you probably already have in your house that can promote your lawn's health. These include: Beer: Beer is actually full of nutrients that feed both the grass and the microbes and bacteria that promote its health. Soda: Soda (NOT diet) contains plenty of sugar that feeds that same microbes with carbohydrates. Soap or Shampoo: This makes the ground more absorptive and receptive to your homemade lawn fertilizers. Just makes sure to stay away from antibacterial soap, as this could kill all those good microbes you've been feeding. Ammonia: Ammonia is made of hydrogen and nitrogen, and plants thrive on nitrogen. Mouthwash: Surprisingly, mouthwash is a great pesticide that won't harm your plants.

How to Make Your Own Lawn Fertilizer

Here are a few simple homemade lawn fertilizer recipes you can probably make without even going to the store (simply mix the ingredients and apply to areas of the lawn): Recipe #1 1 can non-diet soda 1 can beer ½ cup dish soap (NOT antibacterial) ½ cup ammonia ½ cup mouthwash 10 gallons water Recipe #2>/h3> 1 can beer 1 can non-diet soda 1 cup baby shampoo 10 gallons water Recipe #3 16 tbsp. Epsom salts 8 oz. ammonia 8 oz. water Recipe #4 1 can tomato juice ½ cup fabric softener 2 cups water? cup orange juice Spread any of these homemade lawn fertilizers across your lawn once every week or two until you achieve your desired look. Be careful not to over fertilize! Too much of any good thing can be bad, and a buildup of even the best nutrients can harm your lawn.

Tips On Grass Care In Fall

When temperatures cool and the blades of grass stop growing, the roots of the turfgrass continue to grow. That's why grass care in fall includes watering and fertilization to provide the nutrients and moisture the lawn needs to develop strong roots and build a reserve of energy. You can use a hand-held spreader to fertilize a small lawn, but you'll have better control and apply the fertilizer more evenly if you use a walk-behind spreader. Read the fertilizer package instructions and follow them carefully. Make sure you set your equipment to deliver the correct amount. This is one of those cases where more is definitely not better.

Fall is also the best time to apply a broadleaf lawn or moss herbicide should this be necessary. Lawn care during fall includes lawn repair. Fix bald spots with seeds to match the type of grass or a lawn repair mixture. If you've planted a warm season grass, it will brown during the winter. If you don't want to look at an amber lawn until spring, overseed it with perennial ryegrass. Raking leaves is a fall lawn care task that few people look forward too, but it's one of the most important things you'll do for your lawn.

Leaving the leaves on the grass blocks sunlight and encourages diseases. Remember, your grass isn't dead, it's just resting, and it need lots of sunlight. Blowing is easier than raking, but hard raking with a spring-tine lawn rake is good for the lawn because it loosens thatch and scratches the soil. Don't wait until all of the leaves have fallen.

Rain and morning dew stick the leaves together, forming a thick mat that is difficult to loosen and rake. And while we're talking about thatch and soil, dethatching and aerating are also critical parts of lawn care in autumn. In most cases, you'll only need to do this every two years. You can aerate small lawns with a border fork or hollow tiner, pushing them deep into the soil.

For a large lawn, you'll need to rent a gas-powered, walk-behind aerator. They can be expensive, and you may come out ahead hiring a landscaping company to do the job.

Lawn Care in Winter

The most important and active steps in winter lawn care actually take place before winter sets in. As the first frost approaches, gradually lower the blade of your lawnmower with each mowing. This will ease your grass into a shorter length that will discourage damaging rodents from taking shelter in it over winter. Just before the first frost, aerate your lawn to relieve compaction. Then apply a lawn fertilizer. Since activity on the grass will be low, the fertilizer will sit among the blades and slowly seep in, feeding them all season long. When you aerate and fertilize, make sure to move across your lawn in a crisscrossing pattern – if you move in a single set of straight lines, you'll have obvious straight lines of healthy grass in the spring.

Tips on Caring for Winter Lawns

Once these steps have been taken, the key to lawn care in winter is simple maintenance. Sweep away fallen leaves and remove anything sitting on the lawn, such as furniture, toys, or branches. As the season progresses, continue to remove new fallen branches and leaves. The weight of these objects over the course of the winter can kill or seriously stunt your grass. For the same reason, discourage people from walking across the grass. Keep pathways and sidewalks clear of snow and ice to keep people from taking shortcuts across your lawn. Never park a vehicle on the lawn in winter, as it can do serious damage. Salt can undo a lot of the good of winter lawn care. Don't shovel or plow snow that is full of salt onto your grass, and try to use minimal salt near it. If you must use salt, opt for calcium chloride-based mixtures, which are less harmful than sodium chloride-based ones.

How Do I Dispose Of Sod

When you're landscaping, you do a lot of digging and moving. Whether you take out sod to make way for a path or garden, or to start a new lawn from scratch, one question remains: what to do with dug up grass once you've got it. There are a few good options, none of which involve simply throwing it away. Keep reading to learn more about what to do with removed sod. How Do I Dispose of Sod? Don't dispose of it; put it to use instead.

The easiest thing to do with freshly dug sod is to reuse it. If it's in good condition and you have another area that's in need of grass, you can just relocate it. It's important to move quickly, though, preferably within 36 hours, and keep the sod moist and in the shade while it's out of the ground. Clear the new location of vegetation, mix some compost into the topsoil, and wet it thoroughly.

Lay the sod, roots down, and water again. If you don't need new sod anywhere, you can use it as a good base for garden beds. In the spot you want your garden to be, lay the sod grass down and cover it with several inches of good soil. You can plant your garden directly into the soil – over time, the sod underneath will break down and supply your garden with nutrients.

Create a Composting Sod Pile Another popular and very useful way to dispose of sod is to make a composting sod pile. In an out of the way part of your yard, lay down a piece of sod grass. Stack more pieces of sod on top of it, all face down. Wet each piece thoroughly before adding the next.

If your sod is of poor quality and full of thatch, sprinkle some nitrogen rich fertilizer or cotton seed meal between the layers. You can stack the layers as high as six feet. Once your composting sod pile is as high as it's going to be, cover the whole thing in thick black plastic. Weight the edges down against the ground with stones or cinder blocks.

You don't want any light to get in. Let your composting sod pile sit until the following spring and uncover it. Inside, you should find rich compost ready for use.

Signs of Tropical Sod Webworms in Lawns

The pests, which feed exclusively on grass, are the larvae of small moths that you may notice flying around your lawn when disturbed by walking, watering or mowing. The moths themselves don't cause any problems, but they lay their eggs in the surface of the soil. It's the larvae that eat the blades of grass and create tunnels in the thatch. The larvae overwinter in the thatch, then begin feeding on your lawn when the weather gets warm in spring. The pests multiply quickly, producing three or four generations in a season. The first symptoms of tropical sod webworms in lawns, other than the appearance of the moths, include small patches that turn yellow or broth by midsummer. Sunny, dry areas are most susceptible, and the pests aren't usually found in shady spots. The damage spreads quickly, especially during hot, dry weather. Soon, the grass thins and becomes uneven and ragged. You may also notice thin webbing when the grass is dewy. Birds feeding on your lawn more than usual are a good sign of pests, and they are a big help when it comes to tropical sod webworm control. How to Manage Tropical Sod Webworms Controlling tropical sod webworms in the landscape consists of good maintenance. Care for your lawn properly; well-maintained turf is less susceptible to damage. Water and feed regularly, but don't over fertilize, as fast growth may contribute to the infestation. Mow regularly, but don't scalp your lawn. Set your mower to 3 inches (7.6 cm.) and your lawn will be healthier and better able to withstand problems, including pests, drought, heat, and other stresses. Pour a mixture of 1 tablespoon dish soap and 1 gallon of water onto infested patches at a rate of about a gallon per s◻uare yard. You'll see larvae coming to the surface in a few minutes. The soap should kill the pests, but if not, destroy them with a rake. Bacillus thuringiensis (Bt), a natural soil bacterium that works well as a pesticide, usually kills pests and has fewer harmful side effects than chemical products. Repeat every five to seven days Use chemical pesticides only as a last resort and only when you're absolutely sure webworms are present, as toxic chemicals often create more problems by killing beneficial insects. Use products labeled for tropical webworms and don't irrigate for 12 to 24 hours.

Chapter Two

What Is Lawn Aeration and What Does It Do?

Lawn aeration is a techni⬚ue that most people will use at some time or another to keep their lawn looking fresh and healthy year after year. However, at the same time, there are also a lot of people are who are still left wondering what lawn aeration is and what it actually does. This is especially true for people who have looking into a lawn maintenance service for the first time. So what is lawn aeration and what do it do? Here is a ⬚uick overview of the entire process and why is could help your lawn.

What is Lawn Aeration?

There are several different common techniques that are used to aerate your lawn, they all do essentially same thing. Essentially, portions of your soil is removed in small pieces. While it can be done manually, the most common option is a mechanical aerator of one kind or another. Or example, a core aerator will take a 1/2 inch cores of soil and leave them on your lawn. Normally, these holes are several inches, up to 6 inches apart. In its most basic terms, aeration is a way to give your lawn more air. It is commonly used in situations where the lawn is heavily compacted or heavily used.

What Does Lawn Aeration Do?

The entire point of aerating your lawn is to give it more "room to breathe". When your lawn becomes compacted there is less pore space in your soil. This pore space is used both to hold air as well as absorb water. If your lawn is compacted, then the roots of your grass, will not get the necessary oxygen, water, and nutrients that it needs to grow and stay green. In the end, this leads to poor "top growth" and in the long run, your lawn will die.

Do You Need to Aerate Your Lawn?

It can be difficult to decide whether or not your should aerate your lawn, however there are some key indicators that will tell you that it is necessary. If your lawn is heavily used on a regular basis and your grass is looking thin, then you should probably aerate it. Additionally, if your thatch layer is more than.5 inches or your soil is high in clay, then it will likely be necessary as well.

Should Everyone Aerate Their Lawn?

Not every lawn needs to be aerated. The freezing and thawing cycle that naturally occurs, along with earthworm activity will naturally keep your soil loose. Additionally, if you have newly seeded/sodded lawn then you should not aerate it in the the first year.

A Simple Test

If you are not sure whether or not you need to aerate your lawn, the easiest thing to do is to remove a s🞖uare foot section of your lawn (at least 6 inches deep). If the roots of your grass is only an inch or two deep, then your soil might be so compacted that the roots are not allowed to grow any deeper and lawn aeration should be done. However, if your roots are growing deep and looking healthy then you may not need to aerate it at this time.

Ways to lawn aerate your yard

There are two ways to aerate your lawn. One is turf aeration and the other is core aeration.

Turf aeration tools are hand aerator, aeration shoes and spike aerator among others. In turf aeration, you use spikes to poke holes on the soil. Turf lawn aerating will help low traffic lawn to help feed the roots with nutrients, water, and air. This is however not recommended for high traffic lawns because they will add to the compaction problem.

Core aeration on the other hand is beneficial as compared with turf aeration. This is because in caore aeration, you lawn aerate by plugging holes and pulling soil creating a hallow hole where water and air will enter and therefore circulate better. The nutrients will then reach deeper and bigger roots to feeding them.

This does not contribute to the compaction but rather opens up a hole where roots will grow giving your lawn a greener and healthier turf.

Now, let us look at the benefits of lawn aeration. While proper circulation of air and water is important, there are other benefits when you lawn aerate.

- When you aerate your lawn, you improve drainage and reduce water runoff that may cause moss development.

- You reduce soil compaction especially on high traffic lawns. Foot traffic encourages compaction. When the soil is compacted, nutrients, water and air do not circulate properly. Thus, you need to lawn aerate to help the roots get the nutrients it needs.

- Aerate your lawn to control thatch development. When you pokes holes, you break the strands and particles that develop into thatch. If there is a thatch developing in the soil near the roots, you poking holes when you lawn aerate and therefore breaks them and avoids their development.

When you lawn aerates regularly, it will help improve the health of your turf and will avoid diseases and pests including thatch harming your lawn.

You will have to lawn aerate an no-traffic lawn once every other year but for medium to high traffic lawns including those with predisposal to thatch, you will need to lawn aerate twice a year or as often as you feel necessary.

You may not need huge lawn aerating machine as often because turf aeration using spikes may help but once or twice a year, you can perform core aeration for the greater benefit.

The Organic Lawn

Organic lawn care can produce a lush green lawn for your home, campus or business. Now more than ever, homeowners and property managers are concerned about the type of materials such as lawn fertilizer used, but they want to be sure that "going green" does not sacrifice the green of a lush landscape.

Organic lawn care is a win-win situation for the lawn itself. Because it's care methods focus on tackling the root problem instead of using chemical quick fixes, organically managed lawns tend to be healthier, greener, and lusher than conventional lawns.

Its care relies on 1 building the soil that feeds your turf grass using a few basic horticultural techniques that are beneficial to the grass plants, and 2 addressing weed and pest problems without toxic chemicals. Organic lawn care may sound like a challenge, but it is no more of a challenge than, say, watering your lawn with a garden hose. You have to be persistent to avoid problems, but we are fully confident that you can lick your lawn care problems using organic methods. Organic lawn care is easy. You can have a beautiful, healthy lawn without using chemical fertilizers, herbicides and pesticides. You will love knowing that your organic lawn is safe for kids, pets, and the environment. You will also love not having to spend hours every week taking care of it.

A natural lawn is tougher, more drought-resistant, and healthier than a lawn treated with chemical fertilizers and herbicides. By adopting a few simple practices, you can grow a beautiful, green, organic lawn while helping the environment in the process. Going 'green' and using organics for fertilizing and pest control creates a healthier environment for everyone enjoying your yard space. You, guests, pets and especially your children will be healthier for not having had constant contact with potentially harmful chemicals and poisons applied to your organic lawn.

Managed organically, the lawn can be more than simply a green carpet and can contribute to the overall biodiversity and richness of the garden eco-system. Organic lawn care with natural organic feeding promotes expansion of roots and storage of carbohydrates to improve winter hardiness on your landscape. Turf density is enhanced while maintaining excellent fall color and moderate shoot growth.

It is not just limited to summer, it is important to continue lawn maintenance into fall to ensure a healthy green lawn in spring.

Applying fall organic fertilizer, proper mowing, and seeding can help keep grass green through winter and prepare it for dormancy.

It cares does not mean you sit back and watch as weeds infiltrate your lawn until dandelion lint covers your sidewalk. Nor does it mean that you need to be out on hands and knees from sunrise until sunset, hand-pulling crabgrass and invasive weeds in order to have the lush green carpet of your neighbors' chemically treated lawns. What organic lawn care does mean is that, with a good lawn care plan and a minimum of work, you can have an attractive addition to your landscape that is safe for both your family and the environment.

Organic/natural lawn fertilizers are the good option against the commercial fertilizers as they take care of your lawn naturally. These fertilizers are eco-friendly and do not pose any threat to human health. Organic lawn fertilizers are generally "slow-releasing", slow release means that organic lawn fertilizers discharge their nutrients over a phase of time and not the whole fertilizing action at once. As the nutrients in organic lawn fertilizers are gradually discharged into the soil, the plant's root looks for them. Allowing them to mat over the uncovered patches, this fact in itself is a helpful method to manage weed growth, as weeds will find no place to grow.

An organic lawn requires aeration when the soil becomes compacted and the grass roots only reach one to two inches into the soil. A lawn that has heavy "thatch" (thatch is the layer of alive and dead grass between the green grass leaves up top and the dirt down below) is also an indication of compacted soil. Lawns that are rich in clay should be aerated more than sandy lawns but either way, aerating once or twice a year is a good idea. Once the lawn soil is aerated, your organic lawn will be much healthier, greener, and lush.

You may not realize it, but proper lawn mowing and lawn watering are more important than anything you apply to your turf. If you cannot or will not water and mow consistently, then you will have trouble in the long run. Infrequent watering of your organic lawn eliminates thatch, too. Thatch is grass reproducing on the surface of the soil in the runner fashion of strawberry plants rather than sending roots down to grow new rhizomes. The result is a thick matting of dry grass throughout your lawn. When this occurs, grass is unable to grow up through the mat and weeds will take over your organic lawn, as there is no healthy grass growth to compete for light and water.

Chapter Three

Lawn Care Tools

Maintaining the beauty and lushness of your lawn has its share of health benefits. For one, it can be a form of exercise and also a stress reliever especially for the hands. In gardening, your hands are at their busiest and most active. Once they get hold of the lawn care tools, the action and fun begins.

Another health benefit derived from engaging in lawn maintenance work is your getting your natural dose of Vitamin D from the sun. This is particularly effective if you work early in the day or towards the end. The warmth of the sun coupled with the fresh smell of raw earth foster a feeling of relaxation.

An Important Lawn Care Tool

The lawn mower is a lawn care tool that is extremely useful. Just imagine what your lawn would look like without benefiting from lawn care tools such as this one. A great many people with large lawns simply find the lawn mower indispensable.

Whether a yard is spacious or not, it has to maintain its beauty and cleanliness with the use of lawn care tools. Lawn mowers are available in many models depending on their functions. The most popular among them are the push mowers, the riding mowers, and the electric mowers.

The size of the lawn is an important determining factor when buying lawn care tools. Do not make abrupt purchases without giving a serious thought to this matter. Large, sprawling lawns would require lawn mowers that are durable. Small ones will benefit from the use of portable lawn care tools.

Never Out Of Style

Despite the emergence of modern lawn care tools, grass shears still remain to be in use by lawn owners. Grass shears are not only beneficial for your lawn. The nerves and muscles of your hands become energized and relaxed at the same time which is good for your health.

Experts say that the act of shearing is even a means of pouring out intense emotions that you might have, such as fury or disappointment, without being physically violent.

Each clipping action releases those negative feelings within you. As a result, you feel good afterward because after you are through using this lawn care tool, you would be so weary to even think about being mad or disappointed.

P a g e | 34

Lawn Care Tools - 3 Things to considering Before Buying

There are many kinds of lawn mower tools and each has its own specific job to perform as far as your garden is concerned.

Before plunging into buying any of these tools, below are three things to consider.

1. Know what specific lawn mower tools you need Only after you have determined which lawn mower tools you need would you be able to address the problem in your garden. On the other hand, if your garden is, not a problem, you should be able to find the correct tool in order to maintain it. Examples of lawn mower tools are as follows:

❖ **Shears**

Shears are basically large scissors. Depending on where you need to trim, a different shear is needed to perform specific jobs. Examples of shears may be grass shears, garden shears, single handed grass shears, long-handled edging shears.

❖ **Rakes**

Falling leaves cause your grass to look patchy and thus an eye sore. It is a must that falling leaves are taken out of your lawn to prevent this. Rakes does this work. There are kinds of rakes that would do the effective job. Examples of which, are leaf rake and spring-tine rake.

❖ **Scarifier**

These are tools needed to remove moss and thatch in your lawn. Thatch is the dead, unsightly material you see in grass that causes those patches. They usually build up on the soils surface just beneath the grass blades which when left unattended will make the grass die. Scarifiers may come powered, thus using electricity or a manual push model.

❖ **Aerator**

If kids play in the lawn, the grass becomes compacted making it difficult to survive because it prevents air and rain to penetrate the soil. Using aerators can bring back air into the soil. They can either be a powered or manual push.

❖ **Edger**

These tools are used to make your lawn neat and straight. They can either be a half moon edger of an edging iron.

2. Check on the Quality and brand Usually, brands carry a distinct quality with them. Always ensure that you buy a reliable brand that would give you the service that you paid for. However, there are inexpensive tools that give you the same quality as those branded tools. Its safer to do some researching.

3. More importantly, the cost. There are lawn mower tools that give you the same Quality at less cost. And there are sites that would offer you affordable but Quality made tools. With the above guidelines, perhaps you could be able to buy the exact lawn mower tools you need ensuring Quality and money worth spent.

Tips for Lawn Care Practices This Autumn

Autumn is here. This means the chilly fall air, freshly baked apple pies, Halloween decorations, shorter days and autumn leaves falling on your lawn. It can certainly be agreed upon that when the leaves fall from the trees, it provides a beautiful scene, but does it hurt lawn care maintenance?

This month, homeowners will be celebrating the fourth annual National Inspect and Protect Week presented by the Responsible Industry for a Sound Environment (RISE). The purpose of this yearly week is to assist homeowners in protecting and defending their homes from unwanted pests, keeping their outdoor areas safe and leave their lawns healthy for the spring.

With cooler temperatures and dreary days transpiring at this time of the year, it's understandable that homeowners may want to refrain from taking care of their lawn and participating in pest control. However, by spending a small amount of time, your home's lawn will look immaculate come to April.

Here are five tips for lawn care practices you can utilize this fall.

❖ **Maintenance Continuation**

Instead of completely giving up on your lawn care because it's October or November, try to mow and water your lawn as usual. What professionals suggest is to modify the mower's blades to its lowest setting for the final few times you mow the lawn before you're completely done for the winter.

❖ Soil Test

Homeowners and lawn care professionals can perform a soil test to evaluate what your lawn needs to maintain growth and ensure green grass in the next few months. This will also facilitate in saving money because you will not persist in purchasing a wide variety of products. By preparing your lawn now, your home's lawn will look amazing by the time everything is reborn.

❖ Rake

Again, it is beautiful to see a lawn full of red and yellow leaves, but this is unhealthy for your lawn. The best idea is to rake regularly because leaves that are not removed will become wet, stick together and then suffocate the grass and possibly even cause fungus to grow if not properly raked.

❖ Fertilizer (again)

If your lawn is already damaged then be sure to add fertilizer with a mixture of nitrogen and potash. This will remedy the damage caused by the summer sun and drought and provide the grass with plenty of nutrients. Later, just before Old Man Winter makes his triumphant return, fertilize your lawn again because it will allow your grass to survive those extreme cold days - professionals really caution the timing.

❖ Special Treatment

All of this is voluntary, but now is the best time to plant trees. Autumn is usually the preferable season for tree growth because they don't enjoy the summer drought. Whatever tree or shrub you want, you can plant a tree now, whether it's redbuds or dogwoods.

Furthermore, punching some holes, otherwise known as creating air pockets, is great for your soil because then it can create and breathe new life into your lawn. This is important to promote lawn growth.

Keeping an eye on your lawn, maintaining it and not being afraid to take care of your lawn in the winter time is crucial to lawn care, especially by the time spring arrives.

How Do You Choose The Right Grass For Your Lawn?

When you've made the decision to overhaul your garden and get a new lawn, it is the perfect time to take a step back and make sure you have the best type of grass. There are trade-offs between durability and the fineness of the grass blades which affect the overall look and feel.

Ask yourself some of the following questions as you start your new lawn project and let the answers guide you to the right type of grass.

- Are you interested in a low maintenance lawn?
- How much time do you enjoy spending on your lawn?
- What kind of usage will you lawn receive?
- How much shade does your land have?

Do you have children and desire a lawn that can be robust, designed for a family, and a low maintenance lawn?

Choosing the right types of grass for the climate where you live is very important if you want to have the best looking lawn possible. Another factor when deciding on the types of grass that will work well for you is the condition of the property where you are planting the grass.

Where do you and your grass live? Knowing your climate will help you to determine what grasses will grow and look the best for your location. You should match this up to how much effort, time, and money do you have to spend on your lawn. Other things to factor in determining the type of grass to plant should include the differences between how the grasses grow, such as creeping or bunch, the appearance of the grass, and the life span - whether perennial or annual. Do you want an exhibit lawn, a multi-use lawn, or just a green lawn that covers the ground for the kids to play on? To achieve a more perfect-looking lawn, you can expect it to require more maintenance. Will your lawn receive a lot of wear and traffic or sports activities. Will, it be a general lawn and/or a lawn cover on wet soil or dry soil? Do you have factors that would limit the choice of grass that can be planted? Some of these factors can include the soil type and pH on your land to shade conditions, and the slope of the lawn area.

Hopefully, the following will help you on the right path to the lawn you want and need.

The Family Lawn

For families with children, play lawns and path lawns may be a good choice. If you desire a children's play area where games such as tennis, softball, and football can be played, you will want to grow lawns of tough grass. Touch rye grass spreads quickly and fills in gaps and it can be using when growing a lawn for utility purposes. The end results of planting this type of grass can be a lush thickness but with the toughness of a utility lawn.

The Keen Gardeners Lawn

Many gardeners and home owners desire to have a neatly edged ornamental lawn that is weed-free, a rich green color, and a neat and uniformed surface. Great looking lawns require mowing and edging several times a month during the growing season. Awareness of aeration and drainage is important depending on the soil conditions of the lawn as well. An organic, more ornamental lawn needs to be mowed more regularly. The keen gardener's lawn is one with more of a general purpose, with a finer grass. This type lawn is more attractive and designed more for looks instead of play, making it less robust. Lawns using very fine grasses make for a amazing looking lawn, but require heavy maintenance and are more fragile.

- **Low Maintenance Lawn**

Some people prefer to have lawns where regular weekly mowing is not necessary. A rougher utility lawn can be mowed a few times before and after the summer resting period. This type of lawn could only require mowing four to six times a year. Finer grasses will diminish and courser grasses will take control. The type of grass seed you need can be shade, sub, drought, or fire resistant grass, and can be mixed to be specially formulated for lawns that grow in specific situations or for specific uses. There are grass seed mixes for lawns on exposed coasts, tough utility lawns, and grazing laws. There are also grass seed mixes for lawns that are in the sun, shade, drought, and damp environments.

- **Cool Climate Grasses**

Cool-climate grasses are best for lawns in the North. In the spring and fall the grass thrives and slows down in the hot months of summer and in the coldest months of the year. Pennington Smart Seed Sun and Shade Mix is a cool-climate grass that needs 30 percent less water and has the best fertilizer performance. Grasses that have a high tolerance to cold temperatures include Bentgrass, Bluegrass, Fescues (fine), Tall Fescue, Zoysiagrass, Bermudagrass, Pensacola Bahiagrass, and Argentine Bahiagrass.

- **Drought Conditions**

Lack of rain-fall or irrigation can determine what a lawn looks like; some grasses are more tolerant to drought that others. Bermudagrass, Improved Bermuda, Pensacola Bahiagrass, Argentine Bahiagrass, Zoysia Grass, Centipede Grass, and Fescues all have a high tolerance for drought.

- **Warm Climate Grasses**

Warm-climate grasses are used throughout the hotter, more southerly zones; they grow vigorously during the summer and turn browner in the cold months. Many homeowners keep their laws green by over seeding with annual ryegrass at the end of the growing season. Warm season grasses are more tolerant to drought than the cool season ones.

Grasses that can handle high temperatures include Zoysiagrass, Improved Bermuda, Bermudagrass, St. Augustine grass, Argentine Bahiagrass, Pensacola Bahiagrass, Centipede, Fescues, and Kentucky Bluegrass. Bermuda grass is one of the most common types of grass grown in more Southerly latitudes since it is durable and grows well in the heat.

Bermuda grass does not grow well in the shade; it is very soft and fine-bladed grass that is often used in golf greens. This grass works best to plant in the spring. Centipede grass is also a good choice for hot areas. Centipede grass is a light green in color has shallow roots and is subject to drought damage. The great thing about centipede grass is that it grows well even in poor soil; a lawn that has centipede grass is considered a low maintenance lawn. This grass is best planted in spring.

- **Transition Areas**

So what if you live in an area of the country that does not fall neatly into the cool-climate or warm-climate grasses? You may live in an area that is like a belt from the southern half of California or the Northern part of Spain where both cool and warm-climate grasses are found. Tall Fescue is the most common type of grass found in those areas; it works well if a gardener desires to have a green yard throughout the winter.

No matter what kind of climate you live in, what kind of soil you have available, whether you have a lot of time or not much time to spend on your lawn, the one thing is certain - you can have a beautiful lawn that will suit your needs! Start with purchasing one of the right types of grass that has been recommended and get started on having that beautiful lawn today!

Chapter Four

Tips to a Greener, Healthier Lawn

With many people's schedules too busy with work and family, chores such as maintaining the lawn may be neglected. When this happens, the lawn becomes unhealthy and the grass may start to die. A professional lawn maintenance company will need to be called in to restore the lawn's health. They may do this by uprooting all the grass and treating the soil with fertilizers.

There are three main nutrients that are needed for a healthy lawn.

Nitrogen is the nutrient that promotes dark green color and good leaf and blade development.

Phosphorous on the other hand promotes root and rhizome development for the maturity of the plant.

Potassium is the one that gives vigor to the plant and helps in its tolerance against drought and provides hardiness during winter.

❖ Tip One

To determine the amount of nutrients that your lawn needs, you need to have the soil tested, which was what the lawn maintenance men did before replanting grass on my lawn. Even application of fertilizers encourages uniform growth.

❖ Tip Two

Proper watering of the grass is also necessary for a healthy lawn. When your footprints remain on the grass after you have walked on it, then it is time to water it. Do it in the early morning when the evaporation rate is lowest and refrain from watering at night since this might encourage the development of disease causing fungi that can harm the grass.

❖ Tip Three

It is also advised to have the lawn mowed freuently and as high as possible to enable it to take up enough water and moisture.

❖ Tip Four

To cut down on fertilizers, you can leave the clippings on the lawn.

How to Get a Green Lawn

All these instructions on how to get a green lawn and other gardening advice depends on where in the world you live, what climate you have, temperature, sun, rain, snow and so forth. The recommendations is for the northern part of the world such as Canada, USA, Europe, etc where there are "real" winter, spring, summer and autumns. Talk to your garden store about what product to use in your part of the world.

❖ **Spring**

If you have moss in your lawn, never use a machine to get rid of the moss because you actually risk more moss in your lawn the following year. Instead, you can use a pesticide. There are environmentally friendly products to buy. And it is of course possible to use some other water-soluble iron sulfate. When the moss is dead it molders away by itself and is gone in a couple of weeks.

Fertilize - If you have moss it's because your lawn haven't receive adequate nutrition and therefore regular fertilizing is important. When the temperature is about 50 F (10 C) spread out a lawn fertilizer. There are fertilizer for all growing seasons and you can read how often and how much you should use on your lawn. It is often better to use a little more expensive product. You often don't have to fertilize that often with a good product.

Weeds - If you have weeds - There are products that takes care of deep-rooted weeds and at the same time fertilize the lawn. Also here you should be able to find environmentally friendly products in your country. Use the pesticide on your lawn when the temperature is steady over 60 F (15-16 C). The weeds will disappear after about a month and your lawn will get more green and free from the weeds. The treatment often should take place when the weeds are in good growth and the grass is dry and the soil moist. Talk to your garden store about products and how to use them correct.

Weeds - Before And After

Once the weeds have died, after 4-5 weeks, you should mix grass seed and "lawn dress" (soil). Rake out the "soil-seed-mix" over your whole lawn. It will give your lawn even more nutrition and the grass will be even more green, thicker and stronger. You will see results after about 2 weeks. Don't worries about the soil. Both the old and new grass will take over. Also here ask your garden store about this soil products. You can also use a vertical cutter before you spread out the grass seed and soil. Your lawn will love the extra air. If it is necessary make sure you water your lawn. A real "root soaking" (about 30 mm).

❖ **Summer**

Once again spread out a lawn fertilizer. Water the lawn when necessary (about 30 mm). The lawn should be cut at least once a week during the growing season. Do not cut more than a third of the height at a time. The grass can be yellow or brown if you cut it to short right away.

Always use a grass collector when you cut your lawn. Don't leave the clippings on to provide more nutrients to the soil. If you leave all that clippings on your lawn the whole season it will only give you more problems like weeds the following year. Experts often say that the grass should be maintained when you cut your lawn because it fertilizes the lawn. Don't listen to them. Much of the weeds disappear with regular mowing and where you collect the grass and weeds. Spreading of weeds in your lawn is almost not possible if you use a collector and in this program we already use a lawn fertilizer product so we don't need more.

❖ Edge Your Lawn

In May - June, it's also time to edge your lawn with a lawn edger or a shovel. It will improve the beauty of your lawn and garden. It's well worth the time and effort. Edge your lawn as often as you want but about two times in the summer or under the growing season often is enough.

❖ Autumn

Use a moss product again/water-soluble iron sulfate on your lawn. This is if you have any new moss. You will also get some protection against fungal diseases. Give you lawn a "fall fertilizer". (See products in your garden store). This will make your lawn stronger and will manage the winter much better. You should add lime about every two year to replace important calcium and magnesium washed away by heavy autumn and winter rain. Many types of lime can be used to correct this situation. You can use lime in spring or autumn. It is important that you properly rake your lawn in the fall. Try to have the lawn as clean as possible when the winter /snow comes.

If you follow this program, you will be amazed what your lawn will look like in August/September and the next year.

Maintain Your Lawn

Follow the same program again. But of course you can skip the moss and weed products if there are no moss or weeds in your lawn. Also you don't have to mix grass seed and soil and rake it out on your lawn every year but it sure is recommended if you have the determination (and strength) to maintain your lawn green and beautiful.

How To Select The Right Lawn Tractor?

Contemporary country site can differ from hundred square meters up to more widespread areas. Thus when the site is expanded it without doubt will take more efforts for you to look after the spot. You have two ways: go on working in a conventional manner using a raker, a chopper, and a shovel or think about buying very supportive technical gear as a lawn tractor.

It stands to reason that a yard tractor, even if it is a lawn tractor, re uires certain open space for its action. Small holdings may sufficiently decrease its efficiency and would make it look like a tiger in the cage. Medium-sized plots would also be unfriendly to a lawn tractor - owing such plots s it is more preferable to use lawn-mowers and mechanical trimmers. But if your land plot is estimated in tens hundred square meters or in hectares, it is more advisable to get a tractor or a lawn rider.

All lawn tractors can be separated into three groups - multipurpose, garden and compact:

❖ **Multipurpose Tractors**

This type of tractor is used on a site exceeding two hectares: either on homestead lands or on professional athletic fields as well as on the farmlands. The word multipurpose means that this is a extremely powerful device with lots of various nozzles that go with tractor in a kit form.

❖ **Garden Tractors**

These are chiefly developed for mowing of grass, for lawn and garden works and for snow clearance. They also come with a variety of nozzles which allow executing the following works: turning up the soil, disk harrowing, milling, harrowing and other works associated with the soil. Such tractors are fitting for work on land plots of 1-2 hectares.

❖ **Lawn Rider**

These machines are utilized for grass mowing on the territories not above 1 hectare and for snow clearance. Moreover they can optionally be equipped with brushes for sweeping paths, containers for fertilizers and chemicals as may be needed in your monthly lawn care procedures.

What mini lawn tractor can perform for you?

One of the most important functions of a lawn tractor is grass mowing. Thus with the help of any tractor it's likely to make a outstanding lawn. To stay away from collecting a mowed grass by hand, tractors prepared with special grass storage tanks with a range up to 300 liters.

Mini lawn tractor could be used as a "ploughman" but it needs to be equipped with the plough. In the autumn this machine fruitfully copes with fallen leaves with the help of a special nozzle.

Lawn mini-tractor wheels are designed to bring minimal pressure on the grass in order to protect the lawn from ruining. Protectors, in their turn, give good gripping, therefore, a tractor confidently moves both in mud and on a wet grass.

How To Go For A Lawn Mini-Tractor?

When deciding on a particular lawn mini-tractor model the most significant thing that should be taken into consideration is the character of your land plot:

if it is a large one with lots of knolls, bushes and trees, you'll need a more powerful model with a great volume of petrol tank in order to stay away from refueling every hour or so.

if your plot is not that large and trees are planted close to each other, you'll need a lawn mini-tractor with the least turning radius which is very supportive when maneuvering between trees.

It's significant mentioning that the more power the tractor's engine has, the better is the number of attached devices your tractor can use.

Chapter Five

The Best Lawn Fertilizer Results In A Lush And Healthy Lawn

When it comes to improving the look of your lawn, there's really only one place to turn - fertilization. Fertilizing your lawn is the one thing that can turn that brown, patchy grass into a rejuvenated sea of smooth, green blades. So, if you've never had to tend to a lawn before, this task can seem like a piece of cake. Simply go on down to the garden store and pick yourself up a bag of lawn fertilizer. Maybe you'll even go for that brand on sale. After all, fertilizer is all the same, isn't it?

Well, not really.

Applying fertilizer to a lawn involves nothing more than sprinkling it around and letting it penetrate the soil. However, when it comes to getting results from fertilization, that's a whole different ball game. You sees, in order to pick out the best lawn fertilizer that will do the job, you need to first take a real good look at the grass in your yard. The first thing you need to understand is that fertilizer comes in different formulations. These formulations are necessary because all yard grass does not need the same amounts of nutrients. Your lawn may have plenty of nitrogen, but is lacking in a particular mineral. It also helps to know exactly what type of grass is growing in your yard. It may be green in color, but believe it or not, grass comes in different varieties.

One of the best ways to find out the exact condition and needs of your lawn is to have both your soil and grass analyzed by a lab. If you have a local cooperative extension program in your area, you can find out if they will do this for you. Or, you can type "soil sample analysis" into your favorite search engine and follow the instructions. Once you get the results back, you'll be able to take it to your garden store and get some expert advice as to the best lawn fertilizer mixture that matches closely with the analysis report.

While this may all sound time consuming, it's absolutely necessary for you to know what your lawn needs before you make a mistake of putting down the wrong fertilizer. Once it's applied, the fertilizer is going to either be good, or produce bad results. For instance, if you've chosen the wrong formula, you'll notice that there won't be much change in your lawn, or it has even more bald patches than before. When fertilizer doesn't work out, it doesn't mean that your lawn is resistant to all fertilizer, it means you need to figure out the right mix that it needs to thrive.

Once you know which fertilizer to use, your next challenge is to apply the fertilizer as often as needed, and in the right amount. You also need to make sure your lawn is getting enough water during this time. Healthy grass thrives on nutrients, sunlight, and water.

Many people who care about the environment are turning to organic fertilizer in order to avoid certain chemicals that are found in regular fertilizer. This is also something you may wish to research further before making a final selection. There are an few top-rate brands of organic fertilizer that work just as well as the better known national brands. Either way, now that you know that there's more to using fertilizer than just grabbing any old bag, you're going to be able to enjoy a brand new lawn that you'll be proud to show off to others.

Paclobutrazol Information For Lawns

Paclobutrazol is a fungicide that is often used not to kill fungi, but to slow down top growth on plants. This is good for making sturdier, fuller plants and producing fruit more quickly. Keep reading to learn more about paclobutrazol effects and uses. Paclobutrazol Information What is paclobutrazol? Technically, paclobutrazol is a synthetic fungicide. While it can be applied to kill fungi, it is much more commonly used as a plant growth regulator.

Plant growth regulators are used to slow down the top growth of plants, encouraging root growth and thicker, stouter existent growth. This is especially useful in lawns, as it makes the turf thicker and reduces the need for mowing. What Does Paclobutrazol Do? Paclobutrazol works as a plant growth regulator in two ways.

First, it inhibits the plant's ability to produce gibberellic acid, which reduces the plant's cell length. This makes the plant gain height more slowly. Second, it decreases the destruction of abscisic acid, which makes the plant grow more slowly and lose less water.

Basically, it makes the plant stay shorter and stouter for longer. Additional Paclobutrazol Effects Paclobutrazol effects are not limited to growth regulation.

It is, after all, a fungicide, and it can be used as one. Some research has shown that it can actually be used to kill bacteria. It has also been shown to promote richer, greener growth, and to increase a plant's ability to take in nutrients and minerals.

It can be used in lawns to suppress the growth of unwanted bluegrass. Tips for Using Paclobutrazol Paclobutrazol can be absorbed somewhat through the leaves, but it can be taken in much more effectively by a plant's roots. Because of this, it should be applied as a soil drench. It is also included in some fertilizer mixes.

To use paclobutrazol to suppress bluegrass, apply it to your lawn in both the spring and autumn.

Lawn Maintenance Schedule

A lawn maintenance schedule is what you need in order to monitor the cleanliness and greenery of your garden all throughout the year. Many lawn owners usually do not have a regular timetable for trimming their lawn grass. They do it as the need arises, as when the grass is already very long.

Many individuals also perform their lawn maintenance only when the weather permits - that is, when the weather, is neither too cold nor not too hot. However, this is not what a lawn maintenance schedule is all about.

A lawn maintenance schedule begins with a listing down of all the yard tasks that need to be accomplished in one year. Then you need to classify this tasks according to weekly, twice-a-week, or monthly chores.

You should also include data on the length of time required to accomplish each task. This may be based on the previous figures. Otherwise, intelligent estimates would suffice.

Having these in order, you can now proceed with the first item in your lawn maintenance schedule. There may be times when something cannot be completed as scheduled because of unforeseen circumstances such as extreme weather conditions.

This can be remedied by making minor adjustments in your lawn maintenance schedule. The important thing is that what is written in the schedule will be accomplished.

There are points to consider in the preparation of a lawn maintenance schedule - the lawn size, your intense desire to have a well-manicured lawn, and your financial capacity. No matter what kind of lawn maintenance schedule you come up with, the bottom line is that your grass reuires regular trimming.

Scheduling Fertilizer Applications

A lawn maintenance schedule should provide allowances for periodic fertilizer applications. This is assuming that you have allotted time for planting vegetation and flowers.

Likewise, contingent measures for bad weather days should be incorporated in your lawn maintenance schedule. No matter where you are situated, you will experience seasonal weather changes. Being prepared is better than being sorry.

If you have a separate schedule for your house chores, you can use the time of a postponed lawn task for a house chore. For example, trimming grass during rainy days is ⬚uite impossible. You can then make use of this time to organize your garage.

A lawn maintenance schedule, if strictly followed, will serve its best purpose. Things done ahead of time mean more hours for leisure and relaxation.

Thank you for purchasing our book on Lawn Care

If you enjoyed this book be on the look out for more great titles from